MOVE BY MOVE

Move by Move

LIFE LESSONS ON AND OFF THE CHESSBOARD

Maurice Ashley

CHESS GRANDMASTER

CHRONICLE PRISM

Text and photographs copyright © 2024 by Maurice Ashley.

All rights reserved. No part of this book may be reproduced in any form without written permission from the publisher.

Library of Congress Cataloging-in-Publication Data available.

ISBN 978-1-7972-2365-0

Manufactured in the United States of America.

Design by Pamela Geismar.
Typeset in Cormorant Garamond, Brandon Text, and The Seasons.

10 9 8 7 6 5 4 3 2 1

Chronicle books and gifts are available at special quantity discounts to corporations, professional associations, literacy programs, and other organizations. For details and discount information, please contact our premiums department at corporatesales@chroniclebooks.com or at 1-800-759-0190.

CHRONICLE PRISM

Chronicle Prism is an imprint of Chronicle Books LLC
680 Second Street, San Francisco, California 94107

www.chronicleprism.com

I dedicate this book to my late grandmother Irma Cormack and her son Earl Cormack. I hope you're looking on with pride from wherever you are. You are forever missed and will always remain in my heart.

Contents

INTRODUCTION 11

BECOME LIKE A CHILD 17

IT'S A COMPLEX UNIVERSE 27

LEVELS OF ENDLESS LEARNING 37

IMPROVE EVERY DAY 47

DISAGGREGATED LEARNING 55

WINNING AND THE ILLUSION OF MOMENTUM 63

LOSING (BECAUSE YOU *WILL* LOSE) 77

THE POWER OF MISTAKES 87

THE JOYS OF IMPERFECTION 97

THE VIEW FROM THE OTHER SIDE OF THE BOARD 105

OUTRUN THE BEAR 119

SACRIFICE AND RISK 127

FOCUS IS A FULL-TIME JOB 137

START AT THE END 145

TO BECOME, BE 157

ENDGAME 165

ACKNOWLEDGMENTS 171
NOTES 173
ABOUT THE AUTHOR 175

INTRODUCTION

THINKING LIKE a chess player can change your life.

I'm not writing those words just because I've spent more than four decades studying, playing, coaching, and commentating on chess. The 605 million people worldwide who play regularly would agree. School systems in several countries have included chess in their curricula because educators know that the game helps develop analytical and strategic thinking, abstract reasoning, concentration, focus, patience, grit, determination, memory, creativity, self-awareness, and respect for the genius in others. The United Nations has set aside a special day for chess, recognizing July 20 as World Chess Day. Not only does chess promote "fairness, inclusion and mutual respect," the UN said, but it is "one of the most ancient, intellectual and cultural games, with a combination of sport, scientific thinking and elements of art."

These days, everywhere you turn, chess is being used to explain war, business, sports, art, science, personal development, music, and even love. As the runaway popularity of the Netflix series *The Queen's Gambit* has shown, anyone can become enthralled by the subtle mysteries of the game. It's not just high school chess geeks but also actors, musicians, artists, world leaders, and business tycoons who rave about what the game has done to help take their thinking to a higher level. Athletes in particular often attribute a mental edge to playing chess.

Four-time NBA All Star Luka Dončić credits hours of chess playing for his ability to get inside the heads of his opponents on the court. Tennis star and two-time Grand Slam winner Carlos Alcaraz says chess helps him stay one step ahead of the competition. "Chess helps me to be faster mentally, to observe plays, to see the movement you want to make, the strategy. You get lost for a moment and the game is already mixed up." British former professional boxer Nicola Adams, who retired with an undefeated record and held the WBO female flyweight title in 2019, credits chess thinking for her success in the ring.

"Boxing is like chess," says Adams. "You encourage your opponent to make mistakes so you can capitalize on it. People think you get in the ring and see the red mist, but it's not about aggression. Avoiding getting knocked out is tactical."

Despite the now-endless variety of available games and entertainment, chess continues to thrive in the modern era, picking up new converts every year. Instead of being negatively impacted by the digital age, chess seems to be experiencing a revival because of it. Its popularity mushroomed during the COVID-19 pandemic, when social distancing left many of us stuck inside and looking for something fun and interesting to keep our minds sharp. Membership on popular online chess sites tripled at the end of 2020, and a million-dollar online chess tour sprang to life to take advantage of the increased interest. The chess craze has spread like wildfire into America's classrooms, and a recent *Washington Post* headline read, "Teachers nationwide are flummoxed by students' new chess obsession."

Despite the immense audience and appetite for all things chess, there remain those who belittle its importance and try to cast doubt on its relevance. The brilliant mathematician John von Neumann looked down on chess because he claimed that every chess position must always have a single best move, which doesn't mimic the messiness of life. Professional poker player Annie Duke made a similar argument when she stated that unlike poker players, chess players look for certainty in an uncertain world. Controversial business magnate Elon Musk tweeted that while he played chess as a child, he stopped because he found it to be "too simple to be useful in real life," which may be the only example I know of anyone calling chess too simple!

This book will show why those objections are misguided at best, dead wrong at worst. While chess is not a perfect metaphor for life (what game truly could be?), its broad appeal across age, language, background, gender, class, and physical ability speaks to the game's relevance to the way the human mind works. It has endured for more than fifteen hundred years because, as the legendary player Siegbert Tarrasch rightly said, "Chess, like love, like music, has the power to make men happy." And while chess is often seen as intimidatingly complex, the fact that kids as young as three have been learning the game for centuries shows that it's like a language—easier to pick up early in life but achievable and rewarding at any age.

I first fell in love with chess as a fourteen-year-old sophomore at Brooklyn Technical High School. After an easy rout at the hands of a classmate, I came across a chess book in the school library, and my love affair with learning everything I could about the game has not stopped to this day. I've shared the life lessons in this book with players everywhere from New York and Detroit to Kingston and Zanzibar, and I've spoken about the connections between chess and business with companies such as Amazon, Google, and Pinterest. Chess has changed me in fundamental ways, and its eternal truths have helped me navigate the complexities of life's paths in more situations than I could have imagined.

While I believe in the uplifting power of chess "to make people happy," I have also witnessed the transformative power of chess in classrooms and prison cells. Thinking like a chess player can make you a better decision-maker, problem-solver, and strategist. It can help you think before you leap while also trusting your intuition, map out the future while staying firmly rooted in the present, and master yourself while seeing the world through the eyes of others. It is a game that can provide a lifetime of joyful entertainment while also being a serious discipline that can change lives.

Move by Move is a collection of the most compelling lessons chess has taught me. It contains insights on managing chaos and complexity, balancing sacrifices and risks, analyzing backward to solve problems, and embracing imperfection. You'll learn how to build a winner's mentality and how not to be derailed by success. You'll come to understand the most critical elements of strategy and why learning through loss is a key path to greatness. And maybe most important, you'll learn that to get to the top of the mountain, you must first conquer yourself.

I hope these lessons change your life the way they have changed mine.

Become Like a Child

"We don't stop playing because we grow old;
we grow old because we stop playing."

—GEORGE BERNARD SHAW

"If we all could see the world through the eyes of a child, we would see the magic in everything."

—CHEE VAI TANG

Chess is a game of immense beauty. In the hands of the game's greatest maestros, the chess pieces glide across the board in a synchronized dance of geometric and harmonic precision that rivals the eternal revolutions of the planets around the sun. Where others see chaos and complexity, the most skillful chess players see a beautiful tapestry of connected points, intersecting lines, corresponding squares, dancing circles, and invisible triangles. This mathematical order often hides in plain sight; young prodigies can often be identified by their ability to spot patterns that other children—and even many adults—take years to fully grasp. These shapes, sequences, and relationships govern all of the game's greatest tactics and principles, allowing masters to create brilliancies that stand the test of time.

Though chess's beauty is almost endless, it often happens that the better you get at it, the more difficult it becomes to maintain the same level of fascination with the game. Amazing checkmates that cause inexperienced players to go wide-eyed in awe barely register a pulse among experienced veterans who have seen similar patterns countless times before. I have witnessed it time and again in my colleagues; when you know too much, the amazement once felt in the early stages is increasingly infrequent. It's almost a curse, making what used to seem miraculous appear ordinary and predictable. At some point, winning begins to overshadow the process of learning and growing. With limited possibilities for surprise, enthusiasm sometimes wanes.

In early November 1997, almost two decades after first learning chess, I wrote this note to myself:

> *Today I saw a knight again for the first time. I did not know it could do so much! Actually, this all started yesterday as I was stunned by the war that a knight could have against two connected passed pawns. It continued today when I studied how easily a knight could be trapped by an opposing king and knight. To think that such simple mysteries are still*

present on the chessboard stuns me. What game have I been playing for the last seventeen years?

Reading these words so many years later fills me with a twinge of jealousy. This mindset—just prior to my completing the second stage in pursuit of the grandmaster title—allowed me to make a dramatic leap forward as a chess player. I can only vaguely recall the state of mind I was in, that feeling of seeing everything through a beginner's eyes. The chessboard can often inspire that kind of awe, but only if you are ready to receive it. Wonder releases the mind and prepares it for a higher level of awareness. It's no coincidence that I played some of the best chess games of my career around this time.

Elite performers constantly look for ways to cultivate the beginner's mindset. There's a famous anecdote about the eighth world chess champion, Mikhail Tal, visiting beginners' classes in order to get a fresh perspective on chess principles. Imagine one of the game's most creative geniuses sitting among novices who barely know how the pieces move. It would be like Steph Curry, the greatest shooter of all time, walking into a local YMCA to listen to a high school coach explain the proper way to shoot a basketball. Tal's secret to the fountain of youth was to seek inspiration in the game's fundamentals, to see the board again and again as if it were for the very first time.

One of the most astounding examples of an elite performer who consciously retained the beginner's mindset is golf legend Tiger Woods. At one point in his career, when he was winning more tournaments than anyone on the tour, he decided to go back to the drawing board and reinvent his swing. Though he would be reviled by many who thought his stroke was already the purest they had ever seen, Woods, ever the perfectionist, saw small flaws that could not be addressed with tweaks and half measures. He decided to do an extensive overhaul, taking his swing apart piece by piece and replacing it with a completely different approach. Such a radical act from a seasoned professional is akin to a concert violinist deciding to try to learn to play with the opposite hand. "Advanced performers are unconsciously competent," says Bob Rotella, a world-famous golf psychologist. "But any time you make a change, you kind of go back to being a beginner." Tiger's success—and his willingness to risk looking foolish—shows that incredible results are possible when a performer remains perpetually flexible and open to new ideas.

The Zen parable of the empty cup illustrates the importance of having an open mind. In the story, a scholar seeks out a Zen master to learn from. At first, the scholar proudly shows the Zen master all that he knows. After some time, the master pours tea into the scholar's cup until it overflows. Shocked, the scholar angrily asks why the master would spill all the tea. The Zen master replies that the scholar's mind is already so full it cannot accept anything more. If he is to learn, he must let go of his preconceptions and be open to new ideas and experiences.

The beginner's mindset comes naturally to young children. For them, the whole world is a mystery. When my daughter was a toddler, she could often be found hugging a tree as if it were a long-lost friend. In my son's Thomas the Tank Engine phase, he would excitedly yell "Train!" as though a rainbow had suddenly formed in the clear blue sky. A similar thing happened with planes, bugs, dogs, cats, and the garden hose. I'm reminded of a Bible verse that says something to the effect of, "You must become like a child to enter into the kingdom of heaven." Seeing a baby squeal in delight at their mother playing peekaboo makes me wonder if even heaven could provide more bliss.

Cell phones, flat-screen TVs, the internet, electric cars, and drones are just a few accessories of modern life that would have seemed like science fiction inventions forty years ago. Modern miracles are all around us, but overexposure makes us take them for granted. There is a saying: "There are two ways to live your life. One is as though nothing is a miracle. The other is as though everything is a miracle."

To prime ourselves to learn like a child means recognizing that, as adults, we often forget how wondrous things are. It need not be that way. As therapist Wayne Dyer wrote: "To be more childlike, you don't have to give up being an adult. The fully integrated person is capable of being both an adult and a child simultaneously. Recapture the childlike feelings of wide-eyed excitement, spontaneous appreciation, cutting loose, and being full of awe and wonder at this magnificent universe."

An effective way to rekindle a sense of wonder is to take a step away from anything that has become routine. I sometimes take time away from the chessboard. When I return, the pieces look a bit like alien artifacts, and I feel a twinge of excitement, like I'm about to flirt with a beautiful stranger. The game welcomes me back. It will open up and reveal a shining mystery so bright that it amazes and astonishes me. I'll share this new discovery with my friends, and they too will laugh as we are left pondering the infinite mysteries still to be discovered about this ancient game we love.

It's a Complex Universe

> *"If there is only one good move, a great chess player will find it. The problem arises when there are lots of good moves. Then we get in trouble."*
>
> —LEVON ARONIAN, CHESS GRANDMASTER

> *"The most helpful thing I've learned from chess is to make good decisions based on incomplete data in a limited amount of time."*
>
> —MAGNUS CARLSEN, FORMER WORLD CHESS CHAMPION

> *"Those who say they understand chess, understand nothing."*
>
> —ROBERT HÜBNER, CHESS GRANDMASTER

Mathematician John von Neumann, one of the great geniuses of the twentieth century, said that because chess is a game of perfect information, there must always be one optimal move in every position. He assumed, quite logically, that since all the moves in chess are out in the open for both sides to see (unlike poker, for example), then theoretically a sophisticated-enough algorithm could mathematically solve for a single flawless way to play the game. Thankfully, he was wrong.

The proof as to why is fairly simple. There are countless chess positions where more than one move leads to the exact same result in the same amount of time. An obvious example is when one side may have two or more different ways to deliver a game-ending checkmate. In this case, no one choice is better than any of the others. Even in complex situations, modern computer chess programs have shown that in countless positions there are often a few good options that are roughly equal in value. Chess is so rich that it frequently defies absolutes.

How complex is chess? The numbers boggle the mind. Starting from the initial setup, there are 400 different possible positions after each player makes one move apiece. After two moves, there are 72,084 positions. After three moves, over 9 million. And after four, more than 288 billion different possible positions can arise. According to Claude Shannon, an information theorist, the game tree complexity of chess is estimated at 10 to the 120th power, a number purportedly larger than the number of atoms in the observable universe!

This debunks one of the great myths about chess—that grandmasters routinely calculate five, ten, even twenty moves ahead in every position. Many amateurs denigrate themselves by saying they just can't look far ahead the way the pros do. Given the astronomical numbers, precisely foreseeing the path of a chess game is like predicting the exact weather three weeks from next Tuesday. The possible permutations are just too great for even the most brilliant chess minds to accurately predict.

While top players are sometimes able to imagine various futures on the chessboard, it is not the main skill that separates the elite from all the rest. In the 1940s, '50s and '60s, the Dutch psychologist and chess master Adriaan de Groot conducted a number of groundbreaking experiments on the cognitive processes of strong chess players. One of his most important conclusions was that in any given position, strong players actually tend to look at *fewer* options than their less-accomplished counterparts. This is possible because, through study and experience, masters know which moves are clearly not worth wasting time on and which ones demand their thorough attention. Like most elite thinkers in other fields, top chess players rely much more on understanding and intuition than on rote memorization and calculation. In this way, a chess player resembles a great jazz improviser who doesn't necessarily think about every single note in each moment, but almost instinctively knows which ones will produce beautiful harmonious music.

That doesn't mean that the ability to visualize a tree of future possibilities is not an important skill in chess.

To play well, calculating efficiently and effectively is a prerequisite for success. After I had been studying chess for a few years, I realized that I had the ability to follow an entire game in my head while only reading the moves from a page. When I told my best friend Vincent "Leon" Munro about it, he tested me with my back turned by calling out the moves from a book while he made them on a board. After about ten moves, he asked me to tell him where individual pieces stood. I nailed the location of each piece. Leon and I took this parlor trick to Prospect Park in Brooklyn and quickly hustled one of the players there out of twenty dollars.

Many years later, after I had become a grandmaster, I played ten games simultaneously with a blindfold on, winning all of them. I was surprised to learn that many of my colleagues found this difficult, especially since the record for such exhibitions at the time was a truly astounding forty-eight games. It turns out that many of the specialists who did these blindfolded exhibitions routinely were not among the best players in the world, as their incredible capacity to visualize and recall chess positions is only a part of the key to true chess greatness. Deep understanding and refined intuition, as well as other less tangible qualities, such as determination, resilience, mental (and physical) stamina, coolness under pressure, creativity, and discipline, play a much greater role than memorization in winning at chess. In the rough-and-tumble world of tournament chess, the best players are the ones who perform best when their prepared ideas have not landed a decisive blow, and they have to have to draw on other competitive attributes.

An example of a player with these traits in abundance is the Norwegian Magnus Carlsen, who won the World Chess Championship title in 2013, just shy of his twenty-third birthday. Once dubbed "the Mozart of chess," Carlsen, like many of his peers, has a prodigious memory and a superb ability to calculate. However, it's his fighting qualities and deep insights that separate him from the rest. Former world champion Viswanathan Anand, whom Carlsen upended twice in world championship matches, particularly praised one aspect of his rival's character: his uncanny flexibility.

"Whatever situation you drop him in, his promptness to react is brilliant," says Anand. "If his pre-match strategy didn't work out, he'll find something else."

Flexibility is one of the most difficult qualities to develop in chess and in life. Like a contortionist who can touch her head with the back of her foot, the best thinkers are often those who can easily pivot in any direction depending on the circumstances. It's a quality in short supply in the general population. Behind the cloak of consistency ("If it ain't broke, don't fix it"), most people will choose a path and stick with it, changing course only when disaster is imminent. Inertia and complacency are consistency's close cousins.

Inflexibility gets us in trouble because we generally trust our own thinking in much the same way that we trust a GPS to get us to our destination. But there have been times when even that tried-and-tested technology has gone awry, causing freak accidents along the way. In one such case, a father was driving his wife and two kids through South Brunswick, New Jersey, on a foggy Saturday morning in 2011. At a T-intersection, where the only options were left and right, he opted instead to follow his GPS guidance and go straight. He missed a stop sign, ran over the lip of a curb, and continued for another 100 feet before hitting a house.

This sort of trust in one's internal GPS happens quite often on the chessboard, where even top grandmasters can end up wrecking a beautiful position. In a tournament in Amsterdam in 1956, future world champion Tigran Petrosian was dominating one of his main rivals, David Bronstein. With Bronstein's pieces completely tied up in knots and nothing to do but randomly shuffle a lone knight back and forth, Petrosian calmly got up and went for a stroll around the playing hall. When he returned to the board, he quickly made his next move, only to recoil in horror when Bronstein took his queen with that seemingly aimless knight. He had been so sure of the positive direction of the game that it hadn't occurred to him that maybe something could go spectacularly wrong.

This hard lesson of overconfidence leading to disaster has come for every chess player on the planet. The most dangerous moment, when focus is often lost, is when things are going exceedingly well. When everything seems to be going in our favor, we lose sight of how complicated chess (or life, for that matter) actually is and begin to believe in our own power to control that complexity. Sports teams blow giant leads, surgeons make mistakes on the operating table, and investors lose their life savings. Stand outside any chess tournament hall at the end of a round, and you will frequently hear the complaint, "But I was winning!" Those who do not recognize that uncertainty is a necessary feature of complexity will have to repeat painful lessons time and time again.

How does one go about controlling complexity? As you may have guessed by now, you can't. What is possible is to develop the right state of mind to approach complex situations by being flexible and accepting change as a necessary feature, not a bug. Remain focused and vigilant. Look for underlying patterns in the chaos. Don't look for certainty and single best solutions; instead investigate a few seemingly compelling options, and choose the one that suits your style and personality the best. And finally, above all, stay humble. Having immense knowledge is not as important as keeping your mind open to the infinite possibilities of our complex universe.

Levels of Endless Learning

"That is what learning is. You suddenly understand something you've understood all your life, but in a new way."

—DORIS LESSING

"Live as if you were to die tomorrow. Learn as if you were to live forever."

—UNKNOWN

"It's what you learn after you know it all that counts."

—JOHN WOODEN

In 1995, I had a conversation with chess sensation Judit Polgár that completely transformed my approach to learning. Only nineteen years old at the time, Judit, who was one of a trio of superstar chess-playing sisters, had already established herself as one of the world's top ten players. She had been trained for chess excellence virtually from the womb, and at the age of fifteen years and four months had become world famous after breaking the legendary Bobby Fischer's thirty-three-year record as the youngest grandmaster of all time. Yet despite her ability to routinely demolish many strong grandmasters, she had consistently fallen short against apex predators like Garry Kasparov, Vladimir Kramnik, and Viswanathan Anand. Though she and I were friends, I was among the legions of fans who wanted to see her take the next step forward to thrive against the very best.

Judit and I had sat down for lunch at a restaurant in New York City, and I couldn't help but bring up the topic. "What will it take for you to get to the next level where you can finally start beating these top guys?" I asked. She paused for just a moment before replying, "First of all, you mean *levels*."

My mind exploded.

At the time, I was an international master with aspirations of one day becoming a true world-class player. I was ranked in the top 99.74 percent of all tournament competitors, and although that placed me among the top five hundred or so players on the planet, I was still a long way off from the world's truly elite. I had been devouring books, reviewing games with my coach, and playing in tournaments around the world as I tried to elevate myself to the next level to compete against the very best.

Now here was one of the top ten players in existence telling me that there were actually *multiple* levels of chess skill that kept her from fighting toe to toe with world champions and world championship contenders.

I was so shocked by the statement that I could barely pay attention as she explained how difficult it was to bridge the gaps in opening preparation, middle game understanding, endgame knowledge, and competitive insights. At that moment, it instantly became clear to me that not only was there a vast chasm between her and the very best players, but that the gap between the two of us was greater in ways I could only imagine. It felt as if she could see the number pi racing off beyond a thousand places, while I simply saw it as 3.14.

What I learned in that brief exchange is reflected in the old Socratic saying, "The more I know, the more I realize I know nothing." In the learning process, there are literally infinite levels of understanding. Even today, people are confused to hear that as a grandmaster, I only know a tiny fraction of the vast totality of chess knowledge. No one on Earth knows even 10 percent of what there is to know about chess, not even the world champion. To become a grandmaster is to rise to the level of an advanced beginner.

To understand this better, we have to examine the learning process in chess. First, players learn how the pieces move and the basic ways they interact with the opponent's pieces when making threats, capturing, defending, checking, and checkmating. We soon recognize the importance of not giving away pieces for no reason (what chess players call "losing material") since a bigger army usually defeats a smaller one. We begin to appreciate that controlling the center of the board gives our pieces more mobility and more space to restrict and dominate the other side's pieces. We learn, sometimes through painful defeats, to get our king castled early because a king stuck in the middle can easily become a target. We also learn not to bring out our queen too soon, because our opponent's less-valuable pieces will gladly attack it. In addition to these basic principles, we begin to absorb hundreds of checkmating patterns and basic endgame positions that repeat themselves over and over again. This standard repository of chess knowledge has been building up for centuries, and it takes years to master all of it.

However, a paradox soon arises. While the principles are logical, refined, and tested, there comes a point where they come in conflict with one another. Sometimes, it's important to leave the king in the middle of the board to gain time for an attack. Sometimes, losing time by bringing out your queen allows you to win a valuable pawn. Often it's a good idea to allow your front line of pawns to be weakened because you'll gain a key open line for your rooks to march into enemy territory. The chess master has to become a keen judge of how to reconcile these competing principles at any given moment or to spot when an exception should be the rule. To feel these moments demands we take our knowledge and step outside it, to see the game with another pair of eyes. Normally, this happens after we do a thorough review of games we have recently lost, when deep postgame analysis often reveals that we were mechanically following general principles as though they were fixed rules.

This fluid nature of knowledge is true of all fields. For centuries, most thought the Earth was flat until Magellan circumnavigated the globe. Newton's Law of Gravitation was scientific dogma for hundreds of years until Einstein's General Theory of Relativity shook its very foundations. Pluto's categorical demotion made generations of students rethink the meaning of the word *planet* (and learn a new mnemonic: My Very Educated Mother Just Served Us Noodles). Many so-called facts have an expiration date that arrives when we least expect it. In the art of true learning, the ability to unlearn can be the most powerful skill.

This flexibility is how consistent growth happens: New data is learned, applied, and then modified by feedback, which then opens up new thought processes to learn, reinterpret, and synthesize new ideas. This new knowledge is rearranged endlessly as we continue up the winding path to higher levels of enlightenment. We learn, relearn, and unlearn in an everlasting loop. The best chess players in the world do not pretend to know and understand everything. Absolute certainty is often a sure sign of ignorance.

All knowledge is partial, most of it hidden behind a curtain that opens to reveal even more curtains. Answers may seem to be right in front of us, but we can't quite perceive them, similar to how scientists have surmised the existence of dark matter and dark energy but are unable to identify their properties. The possibilities of chess are practically infinite, with the prowess of the best players paling in comparison to that of the best programs, and today's seemingly invincible chess machines will similarly be no match for the next generation of AI. Maybe chess is a puzzle that cannot be solved by any computing power, and even if it eventually is, it's possible that our minds won't be able to fully understand the solution. We have trouble accepting that this could be true, so the search continues for what's behind the next curtain. One thing is certain: We don't know what we don't know. We stay humble inside the sixty-four squares and patiently strive to get to the next level on the staircase to never-ending growth.

Improve
Every Day

> "There is nothing noble in being superior to some other man. The true nobility is in being superior to your previous self."
>
> —W. L. SHELDON

> "We are what we repeatedly do. Excellence, then, is not an act, but a habit."
>
> —WILL DURANT

> "People often say that motivation doesn't last. Well, neither does bathing—that's why we recommend it daily."
>
> —ZIG ZIGLAR

In the early 1870s, an Austrian chess player named Wilhelm Steinitz radically changed the chess world forever. At the time, most of the game's elite competitors played in the spirit of the so-called Romantic School, which preached the principle of going for an all-out attack as quickly as possible in order to gain the upper hand. However, Steinitz, who had successfully used this hyperaggressive approach in the early part of his career, came to realize that these premature assaults only succeeded when met with poor defense. His extensive analysis of the games of the masters proved to him that a far more effective strategy was to build up one's forces patiently so that once the final battle was eventually waged, one had on hand as many pieces and pawns as possible to overwhelm the enemy's resistance.

His theory came to be known as the Theory of the Accumulation of Small Advantages, or simply Accumulation Theory. The logic behind it was impeccable: At the beginning of a game, both sides have the same number of forces with no advantage in position. Though the player with the white pieces moves first, correct play by both sides should maintain the equilibrium and lead to a drawn game. Only a mistake should disturb the balance in favor of one side, which means that even brilliant attacks, insufficiently prepared, will fail against proper defense. With that in mind, the wise player should refrain from attacking too soon, choosing instead to gain small advantages in different areas until the opponent makes a critical mistake. Only then will it be time to attack, and it is imperative to do so since the advantage might evaporate.

When Steinitz first started to use this new strategy, his colleagues derided him, calling such slow buildups "cowardly." It didn't help his cause that he sometimes played highly provocative moves to goad his bloodthirsty opposition into attacking too soon. It wasn't until Steinitz began to completely dominate the opposition, eventually winning the first official world championship match in 1886, that his strategies began to take hold. Today, he is known as the father of modern chess, and the vast majority of his ideas are still used by the world's best players.

More than a hundred years after Steinitz first posited Accumulation Theory, Masaaki Imai, a Japanese organizational theorist and management consultant, transformed business process management in the West by publishing the book *Kaizen: The Key to Japan's Competitive Success* (1986). The concept of kaizen, Japanese for "improvement" or "change for the best," rests on the idea of continuous incremental improvement as opposed to immediate drastic change. Much like Accumulation Theory, the kaizen method of small steps to achieve gigantic growth encourages organizations to play the long game—slow and steady wins the race—with a readiness to abolish old, traditional concepts that have outlived their usefulness. Steinitz most definitely would have approved.

We can use the twin concepts of Accumulation Theory and kaizen in our everyday lives. While many people go overboard with strenuous workouts or employ crash diets in the hope of seeing immediate changes to their body, experts note that consistently exercising a little every day along with a gradual shift to healthy food choices will result in more lasting results. In finance, get-rich-quick schemes usually lose out to more patient strategies. In his bestselling book *Atomic Habits*, author James Clear coins his own term, *the aggregation of marginal gains*, to describe these commonsense approaches: "Improving by 1 percent isn't particularly notable—sometimes it isn't even noticeable—but it can be far more meaningful, especially in the long run. The difference a tiny improvement can make over time is astounding. Here's how the math works out: If you can get 1 percent better each day for one year, you'll end up thirty-seven times better by the time you're done."

Accumulation Theory and its sister ideas are so obviously powerful that one has to wonder why everyone doesn't follow their core principles of slow but steady improvement. The truth is we live in an age of instant gratification, when building lifelong habits of hard work, patience, and consistency don't seem to be as appealing. While we may sometimes be able to see amazing results with flashier methods, the gains that do not come through diligence, sacrifice, and determination are often less personally impactful. As Clear writes, "It is . . . easy to overestimate the importance of one defining moment and underestimate the value of making small improvements on a daily basis." Getting the benefits without the effort can actually be counterproductive in the long run.

One of the best ways I've found to prime myself and my loved ones for continuous improvement is to take a few moments at the end of each day to ask, "How did I improve today?" By doing so, we send a powerful message about the importance of becoming better every single day. Verbalizing this question will create a positive feedback loop, as we will soon begin to hold each other accountable for doing what we say we want to prioritize. Once the message is ingrained in a family's culture, daily improvement will become a natural habit. In a world full of the temptations of instant gratification, having the discipline and patience it takes to incrementally improve in one area or another each and every day provides an enormous advantage.

Disaggregated Learning

> "You don't understand anything until you learn it more than one way."
>
> —MARVIN MINSKY

> "Study hard what interests you the most in the most undisciplined, irreverent and original manner possible."
>
> —RICHARD FEYNMAN

One of the most powerful ways chess players improve is through a method known as "disaggregated learning." Like a mechanic disassembling an engine, chess players break down the game into discrete units to study and master. This is an effective tool since in chess, as in many board games, the number of playable pieces will usually be reduced over the course of the game to create simpler situations at the end, with just a few pieces and pawns on the board. This phase is called "the endgame," and mastery of thousands of endgame positions is one of the prerequisites of any player who aspires to chess greatness.

Most amateurs hate studying endgames because they consider them simple and boring to learn. Instead, they prefer to study openings, in the hopes that they will quickly catch their opponent unawares with some novel move or trap that they learned from the latest book or online course. However, while opening fads come and go, the deep understanding gained from the study of endgames lasts forever. It's no wonder the great Cuban genius and third-ever world champion José Raúl Capablanca wrote, "In order to improve your game, you must study the endgame before everything else, for whereas the endings can be studied and mastered by themselves, the middle game and the opening must be studied in relation to the endgame."

Take a seemingly simple endgame where there are just two kings and one pawn on the board—as basic an endgame position as there is. But the nuances of these types of positions must be mastered perfectly, for all the core principles involved within them. There are literally hundreds if not a few thousand similar basic endgame setups that every self-respecting player should study for the many insights they reveal. To know the endgame is to know the microcosmic truth of chess. The endgame is to the chess master what the periodic table is to the chemist.

Disaggregated learning is used any time skills are practiced out of context. The basic idea is to design games or activities that use the tools of a game, sport, or profession in ways that one may never use during an actual performance. If you've ever watched four-time NBA champion Steph Curry intently dribble two basketballs at once, you will know what I mean. He'll never have to use this exact skill while playing, but he practices it anyway, because the exercise gives him tangible benefits in terms of coordination, facility with both hands, a sense of connectivity to the basketball, and supreme confidence when he's dribbling only one ball.

The same benefits apply when a hibachi chef spins a sharp knife in the air, a martial artist breaks boards with her bare hands, or a soccer player juggles a ball for as long as he can without letting it touch the ground. The seeming lack of real-life usefulness of these exercises completely misses their point. The resulting increased physical coordination can only be a good thing, and the confidence practitioners gain from knowing that they are in complete control of the tools of their trade is priceless.

In my app, Maurice Ashley Teaches Chess, I teach beginners the rules of the game by using exercises I call Skill Builders. In a puzzle called Pawn Mower, a piece attempts to capture a number of opposing pawns consecutively. There are two caveats: One is that the pawns do not move at all. The piece gets to eat them as though it's a hungry mouse nibbling on little blocks of cheese. The second is that every time the piece moves, it must capture a pawn. It may not move to an empty square. This makes it such that there is only one solution to the exercise.

At first glance, this exercise may seem irrelevant. In an actual game, a player is not allowed to capture multiple pieces and pawns in a row the way one might in checkers. However, there's a method to the madness. As the number of pawns grows, it becomes harder and harder to visualize the single path that is the unique solution to each of these puzzles. Not only is the game reinforcing how the piece moves, but students are already learning how to think multiple steps ahead, a skill that will come in handy once they start playing actual games.

Practicing skills out of context can be used in just about any learning environment. My friend Anna told me of an exercise a tennis coach did with her when she was only three years old. He had her turn her back to him, and when he tossed the ball in her direction and yelled "Now!" she had to spin around and quickly hit it back to him. She jokingly recalls how she was mad at him for making her face the other way, but now admits it was a brilliant exercise for training her reflexes, footwork, timing, and anticipation. The genius of this simple exercise is that even a professional tennis player could benefit from it.

Disaggregated learning applies at any age and any level of complexity. The key is to free our minds from being prisoners to the practical. Be ready to be called unorthodox or even silly for trying strange or seemingly bizarre ideas. In the wise words of the great poet Muriel Strode, "I will not follow where the path may lead, but I will go where there is no path, and I will leave a trail."

Winning and the Illusion of Momentum

"Winning can convince you everything is fine even if you are on the brink of disaster."

—GARRY KASPAROV, THIRTEENTH WORLD CHESS CHAMPION

"The road to success is always under construction."

—LILY TOMLIN

One of the most important qualities of a top chess player is the mental toughness needed to maintain focus over the entire stretch of a game. Grandmasters understand that while it's important to start strong, it's rare that a game is won from opening preparation alone. The problems usually arise after an auspicious beginning, especially when things are going *too* well. It's right at that moment of ease when energy and focus tend to slip, and we begin to feel that a positive result may be preordained. But a simple lapse in concentration is all an opponent needs to flip the game on its head, leaving us wondering what happened to our beautiful position.

We've all seen games with huge early leads that came crashing down as the myth of momentum failed to carry the front-runners to the finish line. Inevitable momentum is an illusion, a story that the human mind tells itself when things are going well. Many may argue that momentum is real, that it is a proven scientific phenomenon, and sure, it is quite real if you are a snowball rolling down a hill. However, in the crucible of competition, where the opposition refuses to melt in the face of relentless pressure, momentum can evaporate in an instant. Take a look at the greatest competitors. When they are losing, when they are backed into a corner and it looks as if they may be finished, they shake off the myth of the opponent being predestined to win and find a way to turn things around time and time again.

One such performer, and arguably the greatest quarterback of all time, is Tom Brady. The number of times he took his teams from the edge of a precipice to improbable victory is now mythic. Super Bowl LI was an example. The New England Patriots came out flat and found themselves in a giant three-touchdown hole at the half. With Lady Gaga performing at halftime, there were a million reasons for the long-suffering Atlanta fans to party, as it felt like their team was on the edge of glory. Yet Brady, having already won four Super Bowls, knew the game was not over. He returned in the second half and dissected the opponent's defense like a master chef with a Ginsu knife.

Brady seemed to consciously use the myth of momentum against opposing teams flying high on their feelings of predetermined greatness. His resoluteness in moments when others would be demoralized projected a confidence that defied the moment and the score. By showing that he had clearly not given up, the seeds of doubt started to set in as the other side began to wonder if they might somehow blow their big advantage. Soon, that doubt turned into fear, that fear turned into panic, and before you knew it, Brady left yet another team shell-shocked, wondering how they could possibly have lost.

Chess players deeply understand that your moment of lowest concentration often arises when you have your biggest advantage. The second world champion, Emanuel Lasker, famously said that "the hardest game to win is a won game." Lasker, who reigned at the top for a record twenty-seven years, knew from observation and painful experience that it is when you have the advantage that you must be most vigilant. He was a master psychologist who would often play provocative moves that gave his opponents the impression that they were being given a free ticket to their victory parade. However, it was precisely in those moments when Lasker's vaunted defensive skills would come to the fore, allowing him to turn the game around and leave his opposition muttering to themselves. As chess writer Al Horowitz wrote, "It is axiomatic in chess that it is easier to achieve a winning game than to win it. One bad move nullifies forty good ones, and precision technique is of the essence even when the game is well in hand."

I've personally felt the sting of losing focus in the middle of a game more times than I care to remember (and I'm sure I've managed to forget a few). One of my most painful lessons came during a game against the venerable Grandmaster Robert Byrne during the 1988 World Open chess tournament held at the Adam's Mark hotel in Philadelphia. Byrne, a former US champion and candidate for the World Chess Championship, had represented the United States nine times in Chess Olympiads from 1952 to 1976 and had won seven medals for his fantastic performances. He was a well-respected chess columnist for the *New York Times*, and as a New Yorker, I never failed to buy the Tuesday paper to carefully study his latest article. Though he was past his prime at sixty years old when we played, I knew full well that legends like Byrne do not go down without a fight.

This knowledge notwithstanding, I was delighted when my opponent made an uncharacteristically large mistake during the opening phase of our game, which allowed me to start a brutal attack against his king. My moves came like lasers, and despite having the black pieces (with the disadvantage of moving second), I had a decisive advantage after only twenty-one moves. With momentum clearly trending in my favor, I got up from the board and started to strut confidently around the playing hall. My good friend Natasha Us saw the Cheshire Cat smile on my face and asked me what was going on.

"I'm killing him," I replied. "This game is so beautiful; it's going to be published in the *Informant*." Her eyes widened, knowing that I was referring to a biannual publication known for publishing top-quality games cherry-picked from those played by the world's chess masters in the previous months. She walked over to my board, saw that I was indeed doing well, and with a slightly bemused smile, went back to her own game. I continued strolling around as Byrne squirmed in his chair trying to find a way out. My mind was already on what I would have for dinner.

Finally, my opponent moved, and I calmly ambled back to my chair. It didn't take me long to bang down what I thought was the winning riposte. To my horror, it turned out that my move was not a winning one at all, and in fact I had completely thrown away the massive advantage I once had. Byrne, noticing his good fortune, perked up in his chair and proceeded to fight like a man possessed. Now it was my turn to duck and dodge bullets, all the while trying to suppress the bitter disappointment I felt at tossing away what felt like a sure win. He prodded and squeezed my position for the next few hours, waiting for me to crack under the relentless pressure. After a staunch defense, I began to realize that I had managed to survive the worst, and the position was now fairly equal with no real winning chances for either side. When I could see that I was perfectly safe, I offered him a draw. To my surprise, Byrne instantly declined. In his mind, he was the aggressor with all the momentum firmly in his hands. Even though his winning chances had evaporated, he couldn't properly evaluate the reality staring back at him from the chessboard.

His next move was a blunder of massive proportions. His undue optimism proved costly, as his move allowed me an opening for a devastating counterstrike that won his queen. In total shock, he resigned soon after.

Though I had won the game, some part of me felt as though I had lost. My joy had been tempered by the hours of suffering I had to endure from what had been such a magnificent start. It didn't help when my friend Emory Tate walked up to me right after the game had concluded and pointed out that I had missed a crushing blow that would have ended matters many moves earlier. The winning move happened to be at the precise moment when I had smugly returned to the board after walking around fantasizing about my own brilliance and dreaming about seeing it showcased in print. This game was never published.

Even the world's truly elite players can easily fall victim to the giddiness that comes when things seem to be going their way. Former world champion Magnus Carlsen had just such a moment during round 7 of the 2018 Sinquefield Cup, one of the most prestigious tournaments on the circuit. In the run-up to the game, Carlsen had not been his usual dominating self, failing to win a top-tier event in over a year. The whispers started to get louder that he might have lost his touch and that his main rivals were quite possibly closing the gap to threaten his status as the top player on the planet. In this particular game, the Norwegian was pitted against the American Fabiano Caruana, who at the time was ranked number two on the ratings list. Fabi, as he is affectionately known, had recently qualified to compete against the champion in a match for the world title later in the year. All eyes were on this game to see if it might be a preview of a changing of the guard.

At one point, Caruana made a critical mistake, allowing Carlsen to gain an overwhelming advantage. The position seemed so crushing that the champ decided to take a stroll into a private, cordoned-off area humorously called "the confessional booth." It was a space where players could express their thoughts about the game in progress to a one-way camera, which beamed them out to a viewing audience eager to soak up every word.

Carlsen was not one to enter the confessional booth often, so when he did, the commentators—myself included—got very excited. However, instead of saying a word, the champ simply put his index finger to his lips for approximately three seconds in the universally accepted sports gesture of quieting the haters. His meaning was clear: He knew he was about to destroy his closest rival, Caruana, who at that point was also leading the tournament. His confidence in the direction the game was going was so high that he felt he could let the whole world know it.

Unfortunately for him, however, things didn't work out as planned. Upon returning to the board, he proceeded to make a serious mistake that breathed new life into Caruana's position. In the space of one move, the game took a drastic turn, and just a few moves later, Carlsen had to concede a draw to his opponent. When he appeared for the postgame interview, he seemed befuddled as to how he could have let such a gigantic opportunity slip through his fingers.

"I was absolutely sure I was winning," he said emphatically. "The problem is in all my games, I'm not being practical. I just can't make up my mind. I just can't follow my intuition (and) make decisions. It's frustrating, for sure."

To overcome our natural tendency toward the momentum myth, we need to mentally train ourselves to not get over-elated when we have a big lead. In the quarterfinals of the 2022 FIFA World Cup in Qatar, Brazil took the lead against Croatia on a brilliant goal by their superstar forward, Neymar, late in the match. The Brazilian fans cheered loudly, and the commentators completely wrote off the opposing team. But with only three minutes left to go, Croatia, an unlikely soccer power that had gone to the previous finals with their never-say-die attitude, scored the tying goal. They would later go on to win the match on penalty kicks. Even a perennial superpower like five-time World Cup winner Brazil is not immune to the lure of momentum and can be taken down when they prematurely believe in inevitable victory.

Don't believe your own hype, and don't treat trends as foregone conclusions. Be both the least excited and the most desperate person in the room when things are going well. Treat every phase of a game or situation as a separate entity. Whether it's the fourth quarter, the ninth inning, or the opening, middle game, or endgame, focus on performing your best in each phase, never taking your foot off the gas. Not only should you avoid believing in the illusion of momentum, but you can actually use it in your favor—if your competition believes you are doing well because of momentum, don't argue with them! Never forget that it's not how you start but how you finish that counts.

Losing (Because You *Will* Lose)

> "You may learn much more from a game you lose than from a game you win. You will have to lose hundreds of games before becoming a good player."
>
> —JOSÉ RAÚL CAPABLANCA, THIRD WORLD CHESS CHAMPION

> "I really think a champion is defined not by their wins but by how they can recover when they fall."
>
> —SERENA WILLIAMS

> "I think you need to be able to recover [from losing] to be good. The worst thing in general is when your failure one day affects the next day."
>
> —ANISH GIRI, CHESS GRANDMASTER

> "What is defeat? Nothing but education—nothing but the first step to something better."
>
> —WENDELL PHILLIPS

No one likes to lose. Yet how we handle our losses is one of the most powerful measures of our eventual success. Those who react badly after a loss, who pout, kick, scream, and throw things, generally get no benefit from the experience. The great champions often look at losing as a way to gain precious competitive insights so they can raise their game to new levels. Losing, much more so than winning, can be a catapult launching your game to new heights.

The late, great Kobe Bryant was once asked, "What does losing feel like to you?" His reply: "It's exciting... because it means you have different ways to get better. There's certain weaknesses that were exposed that you need to shore up.... It sucks to lose, but at the same time the answers are there if you just look at them."

I recall playing matches against one of my best friends and biggest rivals, the late Ronald Simpson. Ronnie was a tactical wizard who could conjure up amazing attacking ideas out of thin air. We would play hours of Blitz at the City College chess club in Harlem, and he would leave my ego battered and bruised with the terrible beatings he used to inflict on me. Often, he would make moves that I suspected were unsound, but every time I tried to punish them, he would hit me with a brutal blow that would shatter my position to pieces. To make matters worse, it was so easy for him to defeat me that he would give me time odds: He would take two minutes on the clock to my five and beat me with time to spare. Each day after I lost to him, I would take the long train ride home to Brooklyn, frustrated and humiliated.

After weeks of getting slapped around, I finally came up with a plan. I knew that Ronnie's ability to spot tactics was far superior to mine, but before I addressed that problem, I wanted to understand deeply the fundamental weaknesses behind his moves. That meant I had to gain a more nuanced appreciation of *both* strategy and tactics. While strategic understanding and maneuvering (what chess players call "positional play") help you see and feel when moves might not be quite right, tactical motifs are the moves a player uses to take advantage of a good situation. Think of a boxer strategically cutting off the center of the ring, taking their opponent to the ropes, and relentlessly pounding the body to weaken resistance. That's all well and good, but it's the tactical combo of jab, jab, hook followed by the vicious uppercut that will send the opponent to the canvas. Ronnie was brilliant at spotting and executing those kinds of knockout moves, and I had to be equally as good if I was going to fight back. But first came strategy.

I set aside six classic books on chess strategy to study over the next several months, and I pored over them like a general preparing for war. As the weeks went by, I began to see the ways Ronnie's moves exposed his position to potential counterattacks or where he created weaknesses in his pawn formation that could be exploited. At first, these new insights didn't help at all when we played; he still was able to find devilish ways to break down my fortresses or wriggle out of trouble when I thought I had him by the throat. But each time we played, I was able to identify more and more flaws, and I knew there would come a time when I would be able to take advantage and not let him off the hook.

That time came about six months later when I finished my final strategy book and executed the second part of my plan: a comprehensive study of tactics. Every night, I set about solving puzzles culled from famous games that the grandmasters of the past had played. Those puzzles showed how to deliver typical and unusual checkmates and how to pick off an enemy queen or other pieces with precision strikes. It wasn't always easy to visualize the sequences in the more difficult puzzles, but slowly patterns began to emerge, and I started to sense how a particular poor placement of pieces could be exploited with a few deft moves.

After weeks of nonstop study, I walked into the chess club one afternoon, and night had become day. The complexity in my moves had risen to a level that Ronnie simply didn't have enough time on his clock to decipher. When he finally acquiesced and added more time to his clock, we both realized that he could no longer play me in the same cavalier fashion. His raging bull approach ceased to be effective as I speared him again and again, slipping in between the holes in his formation and punching back with the tactics I had learned. I wasn't yet a better player than he was, but I was finally able to fight him on even ground. Thanks to the many losses he had inflicted on me and the lessons I had gratefully taken from them, I was able to elevate my game and reach the level of national master.

The explosive growth one can gain from tough losses is often so profound that it can make losing a gift. Grandmaster Irina Krush, who won the US Women's Championship eight times, credits losing with improving her game: "I used to take losses very badly. Then a wise person told me to celebrate my losses. I know it sounds ridiculous to some, but we can be grateful for our mistakes because we learn a lot more when we lose than when we win."

In an interview that instantly went viral, NBA superstar Giannis Antetokounmpo responded to a reporter's question about whether the season was a failure after his top-seeded team, the Milwaukee Bucks, lost to the bottom-seeded Miami Heat.

"There's no failure in sports," he replied. "There's good days, bad days, some days you are able to be successful—some days you're not. Some days it's your turn, some days it's not your turn. That's what sports is about. You don't always win—some other people are going to win . . . simple as that. We're going to come back next year, try to be better, try to build good habits, try to play better . . . and hopefully we can win a championship."

It's not just in chess or other competitive sports that embracing one's losses can be a net positive. In personal relationships, for example, losing an argument can be a good thing. In his book *How to Have a Beautiful Mind*, Edward de Bono writes, "If you insist on always winning an argument you end up with nothing more than what you started with—except showing off your arguing ability. When you lose an argument, you may well have gained a new point of view."

Despite the many potential benefits of losing, the frailty of our egos often makes it difficult. Even well-meaning loved ones can be unhelpful when their reaction to your losing is less than ideal. There have been a number of painful incidents in the chess world where a parent has been seen screaming at or even hitting a child for losing a game. Of course, toxic parents are seen in all areas of life, but these kinds of incidents remind us that losing gracefully—and gratefully—is an important lesson at any age.

When winners are treated like superheroes, what's often overlooked is how they got to the top only after losing many times—building up the qualities of determination, resiliency, and grit. A famous anonymous quote put it best: "Success is walking from failure to failure with no loss of enthusiasm." Those who treat defeat as a lesson turn into the greatest champions.

The Power of Mistakes

> *"If you're not making some notable mistakes along the way, you're certainly not taking enough business and career chances."*
>
> —SALLIE KRAWCHECK

> *"If I had to live my life again, I'd make the same mistakes, only sooner."*
>
> —TALLULAH BANKHEAD

> *"The blunders are all there on the [chess]board, waiting to be made."*
>
> —SAVIELLY TARTAKOWER

During a chess game, the competitive struggle is filled with many fluctuations, both on the board and in the minds of the combatants. Due to the game's enormous complexity, players can easily get lost trying to calculate and decide among an ocean of complicated options. This often lends itself to uncertainty, stress, fatigue, and indecision. After four or five hours of trying to counter an opponent's many attacks, it becomes easier and easier to miss simple ideas, or even to see ghosts of moves that are not actually possible. Under intense conditions, even the best players in the world are not immune to making simple mistakes that they would never make if they were shown the same position in the quiet of their living rooms.

Today, it's possible to watch chess games online with the aid of an evaluation bar that will constantly judge the accuracy of the moves being played. As the AI ruthlessly and instantaneously indicates that a player has made a mistake, armchair chess fans in chat rooms gleefully comment on the player's sure-to-be-impending retirement. The fact that their own games would reveal more mistakes than bats in a cave doesn't stop them from heaping calumny and condemnation from behind the safety of their keyboards.

This tendency to cast harsh judgment is not limited to chess. One slip of the tongue by a politician will often be fodder for the evening news. Very few companies want to admit to even a small mistake for fear of tanking their stock prices. "Let those who are without sin cast the first stone" certainly doesn't seem to resonate with folks on social media.

The reality is that mistakes are not only normal, but they are to be expected and embraced. While most people castigate themselves for their errors, true chess devotees know that deeply analyzing their mistakes is the best means of improvement. While a one-off mistake may have been a temporary lapse, many mistakes are part of a pattern that may reveal a fundamental misunderstanding of an important idea. Ignoring the mistake will cause you to miss the recurring pattern, thereby leading to a negative cycle that will never be addressed.

In my own practice, it took me a while to discover a propensity to always want to keep my queen on the board, even if the best path was to trade it off for its counterpart on the other side. The queen is by far the best attacking piece, and since my mind was usually attuned to making an all-out assault against the enemy, I viewed any exchange of queens as an agreement between coaches to bench their star players ("I'll bench LeBron if you sit Kobe"). Experienced opponents would note this tendency and exploit it, sometimes forcing a queen trade to defang my aggressive intentions. In the quieter endgames that followed, I would feel like a shark on dry land. It was only after I had finally spotted the pattern that I was able to address it, and even though I still preferred to play aggressively, I learned to better appreciate a different style of play.

Even after identifying a bad habit, there are many reasons why it's difficult to prevent ourselves from making the same mistake over and over again. One of the most pernicious of these is the fact that we are often weakest precisely where we are strongest. The strong skills that allow us to operate effectively in most situations will sometimes blind us in those very same areas. Black chess legend Emory Tate, one of the most creatively brilliant chess players I've ever met, defeated many grandmasters during his tournament career. His uber-aggressive style won him countless spectacular games, but his make-or-break approach sometimes left him vulnerable to subtler strategists, and his extreme risk-taking caused him to suffer an unnecessary number of bad losses. When I pointed out to him that going all in every time was costing him too many games, he caustically responded, "This is how I play." His continued insistence on not learning from his bad games kept him from reaching the highest levels consistent with his talent.

Mistakes are one of the most powerful learning tools we have. They allow us to embrace the opportunity to learn what not to do by providing important though sometimes painful feedback. Mistakes are also a good way to look at ourselves and see the kinds of psychological errors that we tend to make. Poor performers avoid spending time with their mistakes, often trying to forget they ever happened. But professionals know that it is the careful inspection of their mistakes and the reasons behind them that can foster exponential growth. Fortunately, in chess, we record the moves of every tournament game we play. This allows us to study our missteps after each game: to see where we went wrong, note if there is a pattern to the errors we made, and then go about the tough job of trying to fix them in the future.

Legendary figure skater Michelle Kwan is a prime example of embracing mistakes as a critical component of a champion's mindset. Proficiency in figure skating is built on learning from mistakes, as each difficult jump, once mastered, will always be followed by the next, even more challenging one that—at least at first—is guaranteed to leave the skater flat on her rear. Often.

Kwan experienced just such an embarrassment at the 1998 US Figure Skating Championships in Nashville. At just sixteen, she was the number one skater in the world and was expected to easily win her country's title. But disaster struck a few moments into her routine when she missed her second jump so badly that both her hands and knees hit the ice. She would fall two more times in the performance.

Lesser competitors might have been too devastated by such a public failure to return to the ice with confidence. But Kwan knew that mistakes are an integral part of growth: "I could throw in the towel and give up. Or, I could learn from my falls and get better," she said.

And Kwan did indeed get better. In her craft, falling is learning.

"I trained my whole life to do everything in my power not to fall," she said. "But the biggest lesson is not how to avoid falling, but how to train myself to get up and keep going when I do. You have the choice and the strength to get up and try again. And again. And again."

That courage, strength, and resilience in the face of defeat led her to eventually become the most decorated figure skater in US history.

A chess player knows that taking chances, making mistakes, and carefully analyzing the results is the path to greatness. But the truth may be even more transformative: Mistakes are necessary on the path to self-realization. "You have to make mistakes to find out who you aren't," says novelist Anne Lamott. "You take the action, and the insight follows: You don't think your way into becoming yourself."

The path to freedom may lie in making more mistakes. That mindset gives us what Joyce Brothers called "permission to be human." We make the next move, not worrying about mistakes or failure, because we know we will be better, stronger, and more capable on the other side.

The Joys of Imperfection

"The greatest mistake you can make in life is to be continually fearing you will make one."

—**ELBERT HUBBARD**

"If you stumble, make it part of the dance."

—**ANONYMOUS**

Twenty-five years ago, I got into an argument on live television with Grandmaster Raymond Keene of Great Britain. It was in the immediate aftermath of then-world champion Garry Kasparov's shocking defeat to IBM's Deep Blue in the epic 1997 man versus machine match, and both Raymond and I had been invited onto a news program to give our opinions on the future of chess competitions. Raymond insisted that chess between humans was about to be a relic of the past because, more than anything, chess fans want to see the best possible moves, which computers were now clearly capable of executing. I rebutted that competition among humans was definitely not on its last legs since the average fan would not really care if two machines got bragging rights over each other, no matter how accurate the moves. Looking back, I will take the win over my esteemed colleague (even though Keene has probably long since forgotten the discussion). Having bragging rights over a fellow human was my whole point in the first place.

However, the issue is certainly much bigger than simply trying to one-up the competition. One of the great joys of being a fan is watching the struggle between two opposing sides that display incredible skill attained over many years of practice. Hundreds of thousands of people fill arenas around the world every day to see top athletes perform feats of physical (and mental) prowess that the average person can only dream of achieving.

We love to see the great masters who have fine-tuned their craft, whose play at the edge of near perfection fills us with a sense of the sublime normally felt when watching nature produce a brilliant sunset. We would love to see perfection (or as close as possible) in many areas of our lives: from our doctors, pilots, chefs, rocket engineers, and many others. However, part of adjusting to our time on Earth is the stark recognition that life is filled with imperfect moments and that the journey to excellence is strewn with sometimes-painful mistakes.

Of course, a virtuoso piano recital or a gymnast taking flight and nailing a perfect landing also gives us immense joy. Yet despite our awe in watching Simone Biles fly though the air with grace and power, Lionel Messi dance and weave through a slew of confused defenders, or Magnus Carlsen display feats of unbelievable memory, nothing is more compelling than watching a world-class athlete trip, fall, and then *get back up again*. Dropped balls, unforced errors, interceptions, fumbles, turnovers, or poorly placed kicks are all part and parcel of the story that makes for the drama of sports. We want to see if our favorite team or player can rise to the occasion after what seems like a devastating blunder. And if not, whether they will recover from the mental devastation of a loss and do better next time. The list of famous people who have overcome gut-wrenching failures is long: Oprah Winfrey, Bill Gates, Jim Carrey, Michael Jordan, Stephen King, Katy Perry, Walt Disney, and many more. The lesson from these high performers is that embracing errors, learning from them, and bouncing back to perform at one's best is a mindset that makes all the difference.

This way of viewing life can be most elegantly seen in the Japanese philosophy of wabi-sabi, which is rooted in the ideas of finding beauty in imperfection and accepting the natural cycle of growth and decay—a contrast with the classical Greek ideals of perfection so prevalent in the West. The wabi-sabi aesthetic accepts that nothing lasts because life is transient by nature, and it imbues this concept in subtle works of art, poetry, music, architecture, and flower arrangement. The related art of kintsugi ("golden joinery") takes broken pottery and mends it by filling in the cracks with lacquer dusted or mixed with powdered gold, silver, or platinum, reframing the breakage as a valuable—and beautiful—part of the history of the object.

This appreciation of imperfection is one of the reasons why human competition will never die. We, as viewers, see ourselves in the human frailty of the people we are rooting for. It doesn't matter if the performers are professional athletes or kids in little league; we want to see them do well even though—and maybe even because—we know they will sometimes fail and that they will sometimes lose. We respect effort and determination. When we stop expecting perfection and instead simply try to give it all we have at each and every moment, we have a real chance of reaching the highest version of ourselves.

The View from the Other Side of the Board

> *"If you know the enemy and know yourself, you need not fear the result of a hundred battles. If you know yourself but not the enemy, for every victory gained you will also suffer a defeat. If you know neither the enemy nor yourself, you will succumb in every battle."*
>
> —SUN TZU, *THE ART OF WAR*

> "Everyone on Earth, they'd tell us, was carrying around an unseen history, and that alone deserved some tolerance."
>
> —MICHELLE OBAMA, *BECOMING*

> "Until the lions have their own historians, the history of the hunt will always glorify the hunter."
>
> —IGBO PROVERB

The most important element of strategy is knowing your competition. For a chess player, this is second nature. A player might study a future adversary for months before an important match, analyzing strengths, weaknesses, opening preferences, and middle game tendencies. Even in tournaments where you might not have much time to prepare for an opponent, players will quickly review their adversary's games to try to find any intel that might help them formulate a winning strategy.

The argument that it is enough to focus solely on your own improvement is naive at best, foolhardy at worst. If the choice is between knowing yourself and knowing your opponent inside and out, take the latter every time. A former coach of mine, Grandmaster Gregory Kaidanov, used a vivid analogy to explain the importance of carefully studying the opposition. He posed the following scenario: Imagine you are in a duel with someone. You have a chance for a clear shot, but you fail to notice your opening. What would happen? Nothing much. Now imagine your opponent has a clear shot at you, and you fail to notice. What happens now? The funeral director will be preparing your memorial.

Former world champion Magnus Carlsen is a master psychologist when it comes to knowing his opponents. In an interview before his 2021 match in Dubai against the Russian star Ian Nepomniachtchi (better known as Nepo), Carlsen spoke about the mindset of his rival in no uncertain terms:

"I feel that I know very well what his strengths and weaknesses are. . . . He rarely plays well after having lost. . . . I am not going to fall even if I am hit in the face once. Perhaps that will be his biggest challenge, to handle the setbacks that will come, regardless of whether it's a good position he fails to convert, or a game that he should have held to a draw but ends up losing, or opening preparation that goes wrong—that will be a huge challenge for him."

The match itself bore out Carlsen's assessment almost to a *T*. After the first five games were drawn, many commentators, including myself, felt that it was the challenger, Nepo, who was pressing. Carlsen had played speculatively in a couple of moments and should probably have lost at least the second game. Nepo had a strong start in the sixth game, but a couple of bad decisions led to Carlsen taking over the position and proceeding to grind down a win in a 136-move marathon, the longest game ever played in a world championship match.

What followed next was a disaster. Nepo blundered a pawn in game 8, compounded that mistake with an even more shocking blunder of a piece in game 9, and threw away the match with another howler in game 11. No one could have expected the size of the mistakes from a normally brilliant player whose ability to spot fantastic moves was on par with that of the best players on the planet. No one, that is, except Carlsen, who had predicted with uncanny accuracy his opponent's collapse—caused by his lack of calm in the face of losses and mistakes.

Winning a chess game, or winning anything for that matter, is not the only—or even the main—reason why we should seek to understand the viewpoints of those around us. This skill is important for any relationship, whether with our partners, children, friends, or coworkers. Understanding what's happening inside the heads of others is a superpower that is worth cultivating every single day.

This might be entirely obvious, yet the world seems to be suffering from an epidemic of ignoring other people's points of view. Our political life is characterized by one side spewing their predetermined agenda at the other. Televised debates seem to be more about scoring points than actually seeking out a more informed truth. On social media, most people seem to be far more concerned about posting their own ideas than in truly understanding other people's opinions.

Reflect on the last time you've heard a politician or television pundit say in a debate, "You know, that's a great point. I think I was mistaken and you're absolutely right. I'll have to rethink some things." I'm willing to bet that last time was never. A win-at-all-costs culture doesn't reward admitting you're wrong, particularly when a disagreement is public. Changing one's mind is often seen as waffling. Yet it's obvious that if two people are arguing opposite points of view, then they can't both be right (though they could both be wrong!). A truly honest debate in search of the best ways of thinking about an issue should logically lead to someone changing their mind in almost every discussion. The fact that this does not normally happen is an indicator that most minds, even very intelligent ones, are cemented in their own corners. As writer Edward de Bono put it, "Many highly intelligent minds are trapped in poor ideas because they can defend them so very well."

Are chess players somehow immune from this intelligence trap? I can tell you from experience that the answer is "Absolutely not!" In fact, chess players are trained to defend their own position, no matter how terrible, with every strategy and tactic at their disposal. It is very possible to study a game like chess that hinges on understanding and respecting your opponent's best ideas and still come away stubbornly clinging to your own.

Top chess players, though, deeply understand that your opponent can be your greatest teacher. There is nothing more humbling than having your most carefully thought-out plans laid waste in crushing fashion. Competing at the highest level means having an opponent who can identify your mistakes and expose the flaws that led you to make those moves in the first place. Chess is a true testing ground of bold ideas, and a real student of the game wants nothing more than high-level opposition to prove or disprove those ideas so that the truth can be uncovered.

The thirteenth world chess champion, Garry Kasparov, had the good fortune of receiving some of the most brutal lessons in his early career at the hands of his archnemesis, Anatoly Karpov, who once stood between him and the title. Before their epic world championship match in 1984, Kasparov's rise had been meteoric. He had dominated some of the finest players in chess history with his daring and slashing style to such an extent that it seemed that the winds of destiny were whisking him to the very top of the mountain. In his mind, and in the minds of most of us watching, no one could stop him. No one, that is, until he finally faced off against the legendary Karpov.

At only twenty-one years old, the effervescent Kasparov thought that he would pound the veteran Karpov into submission as he had all the others. Except this time, when the match finally began, his attacks proved as effective as trying to punch through a brick wall with your bare knuckles. Karpov, ever the master of anticipating danger, swallowed up all the energy in Kasparov's moves, and then turned to exploiting all the weaknesses left behind. In a flash, the reigning champion had won four out of the first nine games, and with only six wins needed to secure victory, the match seemed like it was over before it had even started.

Stunned by the unexpected turn of events, Kasparov realized that a change of strategy was needed. He decided in desperation to switch to guerrilla warfare, reducing risk and waiting for his best chance to strike. Karpov, in what would prove to be a costly mistake, decided to stick to his risk-free style instead of going in for the kill. The players drew a surreal seventeen games in a row as the match dragged on for months. As Kasparov describes it in his book *How Life Imitates Chess*, "My team and I spent so much time thinking about how Karpov played, which strategies he would employ, that I uncannily felt as if I were becoming Karpov."

This deep dive into his opponent's mind eventually paid off. Although he lost game 27, placing him at the edge of a precipice, the young phenom was finally able to land a blow in game 32. After another nerve-wracking five weeks of drawn games, Kasparov broke through to win games 47 and 48. At this point, the organizers made the controversial decision to put a halt to the match and to reschedule a new one several months later. It didn't matter. Kasparov had learned enough about his opponent, and about his own flaws, that in the return match he won the very first game and eventually the match, securing his first world championship title. He would go on to dominate the chess world for the better part of two decades.

Greatness comes from listening intently to the messages, direct or indirect, that come from others. It is not only the quest for truth that should spur us on, but also an intense curiosity. Why do others think the way they do? What are their most profound wishes and desires? What are they saying with their words, their subtle gestures, and their actions? If we are truly curious about seeing the point of view of others, the world opens up to us in profound and life-changing ways.

For many years, I had held on to some resentment of my father for not being around for a large part of my life. My parents were separated, and I felt his lack of direct presence acutely, especially as I grew into manhood. Despite the fact that we had a loving, respectful relationship, it was a painful feeling I couldn't shake. I would often publicly give credit to my mother and my grandmother for their sacrifices that allowed me to become the man that I am, but I gave no credit to my dad.

I decided one day to confront my father as a way of releasing any feelings of negativity that I had toward him. To my surprise, he replied that he had always been hurt that I had never acknowledged his contributions to my growth and success. I thought he was just being defensive, and I began to push back strongly, but as he spoke, I came to realize that he had indeed contributed in ways great and small. Though we hadn't seen him every day, he had made it a point to have my baby sister and me over regularly on weekends so we could stay connected with him and our half-siblings. He would usually cook us a great meal topped off with his signature banana bread, and then we would play card games and dominoes for hours on end. During those games, he would explain some small tactical or strategic points, the moments during each contest where we may have made a better play along the way. He had a sharp memory, and at the end of a hand he could tell which cards we each held based on how we had played up to that point. He wasn't a great chess player, but he had been teaching me how to think like one all along.

By actively listening to his point of view, I came to understand the impact he had had on my life. He didn't have to explain everything; I just had to have an open and receptive spirit ready to hear him out instead of trying to prove how right I was. Later, I was able to fill in the rest of the story myself. My view of his contributions began to change that day, and it allowed us to become even closer than we already were. Now I can happily say that I am indeed my father's son.

There are a few important qualities you must cultivate to begin to see the world from other viewpoints: An intense curiosity. A desire to deeply understand not only people you like, but those you do not. And a willingness to admit when you are wrong. It may be difficult to name even a handful of people in our lives who embody *all* of these qualities. We should work to ensure that we are at the top of that list.

Outrun the Bear

> "If you can see your path laid out in front of you step by step, you know it's not your path."
>
> —JOSEPH CAMPBELL

> "One doesn't have to play well; it's enough to play better than your opponent."
>
> —SIEGBERT TARRASCH

There is an old, apocryphal story about two hikers who happen upon an angry bear. One calmly kicks off his hiking boots and starts to put on his running shoes. The other hiker looks at him incredulously and says, "Those aren't going to help you outrun the bear." The other replies, "I don't have to outrun the bear. I just have to outrun you."

Chess players use a similar strategy. Most people think that grandmasters routinely analyze twenty moves in advance, and it surprises them to learn that this is simply not true in most cases. When asked by a reporter how many moves ahead he sees, Charles Jaffe, known as the Crown Prince of East Side Chess, replied, "I see only one move ahead, but always the best move."

In 1927, the great Vera Menchik said, "When, for instance, I am asked how many moves I think ahead, I must, if I'm truthful, give the same answer as that of the celebrated Czechoslovakian player Richard Réti: not even one move.... If you find this confession disappointing, and not at all in accord with the general idea of the super brain that all chess players are supposed to have, I can only point out . . . that everyone brought up to the modern style of play relies largely on positional play: that is, on moves which the player regards as *certain to come in useful whatever course the game may actually take*" (emphasis mine).

This idea of "useful moves" makes playing chess a lot easier than it might otherwise be. Trying to calculate absolutely everything is a tortuous, impossible endeavor. The complexity of the game makes this a hopeless task, even for computers that analyze hundreds of millions of positions per minute. To simplify matters to a human scale, it's best to have an overall strategy that is effective enough to make sense no matter what the other side does. That could mean making moves that ensure the king is safe, placing pieces on central squares where they have more mobility, stopping your opponent's main threats, or advancing a strong pawn further down the board. These moves are sure to improve our position as long as we are not making a definite mistake.

There is a famous chess quote, attributed to the great Russian player Mikhail Chigorin, that goes, "Even a poor plan is better than no plan." While this kind of proactive mindset is to be commended, it can also be detrimental if adhered to too firmly. Going back to the "outrun the bear" scenario, imagine if the choices were to have no plan or to charge the bear! (If you trust TikTok, dogs have apparently tried this stunt with pretty decent success, but I know I wouldn't risk it.) Better to let your friend experiment with this while you finish putting on your running shoes.

Lion tracker Renias Mhlongo could have been speaking about chess strategy when he said, "I don't know where we are going, but I know exactly how to get there." There are too many variables in almost any activity to calculate all the details to the finish line. Better to plan one step at a time, knowing which direction makes sense in each moment and going where the trail takes you.

In 1989, I played a game against National Master Daniel Shapiro. I had started an attack against his king and thought I would soon wrap up the game when he suddenly played a stunning queen sacrifice that I had not foreseen. In shock, I had to get my bearings before remembering that since I was the one with a good position, there was no need to panic. I studied the situation and decided not to take his vulnerable queen, but instead to continue with my original attack. Soon, he had to retreat, and shortly thereafter I overwhelmed his position and forced him to resign. By staying one step ahead of my opponent and not being distracted by temptation, I was able to go about winning a memorable game.

Whether it's battles between smartphones, car companies, or political rivals, staying one step ahead is usually a smarter strategy than trying to plan years in advance. When boxer and part-time philosopher Mike Tyson said, "Everyone has a plan until they get punched in the mouth," he was speaking about the need to stay present in the moment while also trying to stay one punch ahead of your rival. Have a plan, but remain flexible enough to trash the plan and do something entirely different if needed. Keep up the pressure until your competitor makes a mistake. It's always better to let someone else try to outrun the bear.

Sacrifice and Risk

"The needs of the many outweigh the needs of the few."

—**SPOCK, *STAR TREK II: THE WRATH OF KHAN***

"If at some point you don't ask yourself, 'What have I gotten myself into?' then you're not doing it right."

—**ROLAND GAU**

The word *sacrifice* is one of the most profound concepts in the human lexicon. Everywhere in the world, across countries, race, gender, ethnicities, and belief systems, the idea of sacrificing something for the greater good has an emotional and spiritual resonance that transcends time and place. The act of sacrifice holds an elevated and sometimes sacred place in societies across the globe.

While sacrifices may be rare in a person's daily life, they happen as a matter of course in a large number of chess games. Many positions cannot be won or saved without something of value being given away, from a lowly pawn all the way up to the mighty queen. Certain types of sacrifices happen so frequently that to an experienced player they might be considered routine, almost boring, and it often takes an unusual sort of sacrifice to quicken the pulse of jaded grandmasters who have seen tens of thousands of them in their lifetimes.

In the introduction to his classic book, *The Art of Sacrifice in Chess*, author and player Rudolf Spielmann wrote, "The beauty of a game of chess is usually appraised, and with good reason, according to the sacrifices it contains. On principle we incline to rate a sacrificial game more highly than a positional game. Instinctively we place the moral value above the scientific. We honor [the more scientific] Capablanca, but our hearts beat higher when [Paul] Morphy's name is mentioned." He goes on to write, "The art of sacrifice is a part of the game that requires a player to have a keen eye, a sensitive touch, and a fearless spirit."

It is this "moral value" requiring a "fearless spirit" that separates some sacrifices from others. Spielmann draws a clear distinction between what he calls a "sham sacrifice" and a real one. A sham sacrifice is one where one can easily see that the piece being given up will return concrete benefits that can be clearly calculated. Any player would be happy to part with their queen if they see that they can checkmate the opponent's king within a couple of moves. However, in the case of a real sacrifice, giving away a piece offers gains that are neither immediate nor tangible. The return on investment might be controlling more space, creating an assailable weakness in the opponent's position, or having more pieces in the critical sector of attack. In chess, we call these intangibles "compensation." Having enough compensation for a sacrificed piece is a judgment call based on knowledge of similar situations or a refined intuitive feel based on thousands of games played. Of course, compensation doesn't guarantee that you will win the game, and if these intangible advantages don't pan out, then that extra material you gifted to the opponent could come roaring back to overwhelm your smaller army.

Life is filled with examples of sham sacrifices versus real ones. When someone takes out a college loan, there is a reasonable assumption that, through future earnings, they will be able not only to pay off the loan, but also to earn more money on top of it. This assumption may not work out, but it has been executed so many times with success that many students feel safe taking on that debt. The fact that it may take years, or in some cases even decades, to see the sacrifice pay off doesn't change the sense of confidence most young people and their families have when investing in education.

In contrast, real sacrifices promise no guarantee of a concrete return. My mother made an incalculably real sacrifice when she made the painful decision to leave my brother, sister, and me in Jamaica, where we're from, to head to the United States in search of a better life. I was only two years old when she left. It would take her ten long years to gain citizenship and be able to sponsor us to join her in this land of opportunity. She could not have known how those ten years would play out and the infinite number of possible challenges we might all have to overcome. In fact, the very first day after she arrived in the United States, Dr. Martin Luther King Jr. was shot and killed in Memphis, setting off riots all around the country. The way she tells it, she was in shock that her dream began in such a devastating fashion. But she understood that this was not just about her emotions and fears; she had three young kids, being taken care of by her mother, who were relying on her to push on. And push on she did, with courage and determination and a sense of purpose, and a decade later she accomplished the task that she had set her mind to so many years before, and finally we were able to reunite as one family.

Her sacrifice came with unanticipated results. While she had dreamt that we would all get a college degree (we did), she assumed that we would end up in traditional professions with guaranteed pension plans. She could not have foreseen that I would end up making my living from chess, that my brother's martial arts addiction would lead to his becoming a three-time kickboxing champion, or that her baby girl would leave the world of business behind to win six world titles in boxing. That her three children would also be Hall of Fame inductees in their respective fields defies any sort of foresight. Her sacrifice, made with good intentions and a willingness to endure supreme struggle, paid off beyond her wildest imagination.

It did not have to turn out that way. It did because she was willing to stomach the key aspect of making real sacrifices: the willingness to take risks.

For a chess player, risk is as much intuited as it is calculated. Due to the inherent complexity of the game, it is virtually impossible to assess with certainty whether a risky move will pay off in the end. It's up to the player to decide if sufficient conditions have been met to take the chance on a risky move. Those conditions may be an aggressive, attacking posture, dominant pieces, weaknesses in your opponent's position, time pressure, or the stress of the competitive situation. All these could add up to a certain degree of confidence in the chance of a positive result.

When it comes to risk, grandmasters are not a monolithic group. Depending on their personalities, top players have different levels of risk tolerance. On one hand, you'll find the swashbuckling, dynamic attacking personality types like Alexander Alekhine, Mikhail Tal, and Rashid Nezhmetdinov, who will take risks without much hesitation. On the other side of the spectrum are more conservative players such as José Raúl Capablanca, Tigran Petrosian, and Wesley So. Tolerance for risk is very personal.

What we do know, however, is that the famous saying "No risk, no reward" is true in many cases. A skilled adversary is normally able to handle solid, conservative play and therefore able rob us of opportunities that may be inherent in our position. As Magnus Carlsen put it: "Not being willing to take risks is an extremely risky strategy."

To be comfortable with risk is to be comfortable with uncertainty. The ninth world champion, Tigran

Petrosian of Armenia, wisely observed that most people who sacrifice play as though they lost the material, not as if they sacrificed it. To take a risk effectively requires being at peace with the consequences and not needing to see a quick return to confirm the correctness of the decision.

Taking a chance doesn't mean there will be a successful outcome, nor does it require it. If the reasons are sound, the risk should be taken almost reflexively. The more often we trust our judgment, the more confidence we gain in our decision-making capacity. The courage to take risks becomes a worthwhile end in itself.

Focus Is a Full-Time Job

"You don't get results by focusing on results. You get results by focusing on the actions that produce results."

—MIKE HAWKINS

"The successful warrior is the average man, with laser-like focus."

—BRUCE LEE

"When you are preparing for a tournament, you have to treat it like the most important event in your life. But while you are playing that game—the most important of your life—that is when you have to just take it easy and just do it."

—VISWANATHAN ANAND,
FIFTEENTH WORLD CHESS CHAMPION

Human beings have a natural tendency to relax when things seem to be going really well. When people's needs have been sufficiently met, it's hard to see mental toughness as an imperative. We like to carve out a comfortable space for ourselves and then return to it again and again and again.

Chess players often suffer from this "sin of complacency." Once we have built up a big enough advantage, our "sloth brain" kicks in and tells us that danger has passed and there is no longer a need to exert maximum effort. What we forget is that the exact opposite is going on inside the opponent's head! They can hear the grim reaper knocking, and every bit of instinct to survive is coursing through their veins to stave off defeat. As Grandmaster Daniel Naroditsky describes it: "It is important to recognize that the defender has nothing to lose. Your opponent will do everything in his power to trick you, prolong the game, or pounce on your fatigue."

Many years ago, I played a game against a lower-ranked opponent. I had made a huge mistake earlier in the game, and he had exploited it masterfully. I was in a seemingly hopeless endgame, two pawns down, with little to no chance of survival. My opponent's eyes were lit up like a kid in a candy store. Defeating a grandmaster is a moment any player cherishes forever.

It was precisely at this moment that I took advantage of my opponent's desire to exhale. Studying the board intently, I noticed the possibility of a devious trap that would stave off defeat. The chance of the play actually working was remote, and it was absurdly easy to stop if my opponent noticed it was coming. Knowing this, I proceeded to do my best Denzel Washington impression and act as though I could see the writing on the wall. I sighed just a touch more deeply, wrote my moves down with a little less care, and stared off into the distance with a look of hopelessness bordering on disgust. Reading my reactions as those of a man heading to the electric chair, my opponent gleefully made all the natural moves that should have forced my resignation.

In his mind, the game was over and there was no longer any need to stay focused, buckle down, sniff out danger, or avoid traps. It wasn't until he made the final natural move that allowed me to sacrifice a rook and force a stalemate that he suddenly realized that he had been tricked. Chess teaches brutally painful lessons.

My opponent's behavior is an example of the principle of least effort. Simply stated, it postulates that in most situations people and animals will choose the path of least resistance. Our brains and bodies naturally seek to conserve energy, and once we ascertain that intense effort is no longer needed to accomplish a goal, we have the tendency to shut down our emergency response systems in order to retain our valuable resources for future activities. There is no need to run at top speed if a light jog will get us to our destination just the same.

Even elite athletes have the tendency to get comfortable, even in the height of competition. The desire to keep playing at full tilt wanes as the goal seems more certain. (There's a reason it's called "a comfortable lead.") One of the most famous examples of this in sports history occurred during the 100-meter finals at the 2008 Olympics in Beijing when legendary Jamaican sprinter Usain Bolt realized he was guaranteed to win gold. What did he do at his moment of triumph? He cruised to the finish line. He won, but calculations show that if he had maintained his speed, he would have clocked in at 9.55 seconds, a world record that would still be standing today.

Is there a way to fight the desire to relax when everything seems to be going well? Sort of. The human mind is constantly looking for ways to make life easier, so your sloth mind will always keep looking for the first exit to its mental sofa. As is often the case, we are our own worst enemy.

Though our awareness of our own tendencies won't necessarily solve the problem, it at least allows us to try to fight against it with whatever tools we can muster. One such technique is to establish when and where we wish to remain hyper-focused. If I'm playing a long chess game, I want to remain in the zone the entire time. It's the same for any athletic competition, musical performance, or sales pitch. This is not the case when I'm speaking to my children, lying on a beach, or salsa dancing for fun. Intense focus and concentration have a time and place.

A second tool is to monitor your overconfidence level. This is very difficult to do on our own, so it's nice to have someone close to us who knows us well and can warn us when we seem to be getting too comfortable. Coaches often call timeout when they can see their team is just going through the motions. It's up to the coach to remind the players of the dangers of complacency and reignite their will to play at full intensity.

One way to do this is to intentionally shift the goalposts by posing additional in-game challenges for yourself or your team. If you have a big lead by the end of the first half, the challenge might be to increase the lead in the second half by the same amount. The Golden State Warriors, led by coach Steve Kerr, have a special knack for flustering their opponents in the third quarter of games by playing with hyper-aggression and a killer mentality as soon as the game restarts. Instead of resting on their laurels, they attack with an increased sense of urgency, as though the game itself were on the line in those first crucial minutes, even though there is a full half remaining. This style of "orchestrated desperation" when it doesn't seem necessary helped them win four NBA titles in eight years.

It's important to note that being hyper-focused is not the opposite of staying loose. Being too tense can kill effectiveness as much as losing focus can. Deep breathing or meditation techniques can calm the mind without causing focus to wane. Staying well hydrated and getting enough rest are also positive ways to prepare the nervous system to maintain energy when the mind just wants to ease up and take a break.

We risk losing all our hard-won gains when we let our focus flag, sometimes for even an instant. The truth lies in the Zen proverb: "When walking, walk. When eating, eat." In today's hyper-distracted times, nothing could be simpler or more difficult.

Start at the End

> "Once you have glimpsed the world as it might be, it is impossible to live anymore complacent in the world as it is."
>
> —ANONYMOUS

> "The strategist starts with a goal in the distant future and works backwards to the present."
>
> —GARRY KASPAROV, THIRTEENTH WORLD CHESS CHAMPION

> "The future ain't what it used to be."
>
> —YOGI BERRA

There is a quote by astronomer Carl Sagan that goes, "You have to know the past to understand the present." While Sagan is unquestionably correct, there is another way to approach history, and one of my favorite quotes about it comes from mathematician and puzzle creator Raymond Smullyan, whose book *The Chess Mysteries of Sherlock Holmes* was one of the most fascinating and enjoyable that I have ever read. It goes, "To know the past, you must first know the future." You may have to read those words a few times.

Smullyan's book explores unusual chess puzzles that can only be solved using retrograde analysis, or backward thinking. Instead of the usual chess puzzle that involves figuring out the best way to proceed from a given position, retro puzzles ask, "Here is where we are—how did we get here?" The answers are hidden inside the position itself, and the solver has to be a detective to work backward in time. Much like forensic analysis might be used to solve a cold case, the exact positioning of a piece or pawn can indicate events that occurred on the chessboard many moves before.

The most interesting retro puzzles are the ones where only the knowledge of future events can help solve what happened in the past. Does one side win the game? Does the game end in a stalemate? Does a pawn make it to the other side of the board and get promoted into a queen? The solver must look for clues in the future because the past or the present cannot provide enough information to properly solve the riddle.

As intriguing as this may be for a chess game, it's interesting to ponder whether there are instances in real life where one needs to know the future to understand something that happened in the past. It turns out that there are many. A simple example is pregnancy. Currently, medical science has no way of establishing if a woman has become pregnant in the seconds after intercourse. There is a special hormone—human chorionic gonadotropin (hCG)—that begins to develop in a woman's body from the moment she conceives. However, this chemical needs at least ten days to build up in the body before it can be detected, which can cause very early pregnancy tests to come back negative. Each day of early pregnancy, the woman's body will continue to create more hCG, which will make it more likely that a pregnancy test will show as positive as the weeks go by. In this case, the past cannot be reliably known until the future properly reveals it.

A significant portion of the science of astronomy is also based on the future revealing the past. The night sky is filled with light that originated millions, even billions, of years ago. Astronomers have no way of knowing that a star exploded in the distant past until its light reaches us at some future time. If our own sun exploded this second, we would only become aware of that cataclysmic event eight minutes and twenty seconds from now. Maybe one day humans will receive a message sent by an alien race eons ago, an instance where our future will collide with their past to unlock the mystery of whether we are alone in the universe.

In an earlier chapter, I wrote about my mother making the extraordinary decision to leave my brother, sister, and me in Jamaica in the care of our grandmother and to pursue a better life for our family in the United States. As a two-year-old, I did not understand what she was doing, nor that she would only be able to see us for just two weeks at a time each year we were separated. As I grew older, I came to resent her absence even though I knew that her every intention was to send for us once she had completed the requirements for obtaining US citizenship. When we finally joined her ten years later, I thought I had forgiven her for leaving. I had not.

Fast-forward seventeen years into the future. I was a grown man of twenty-nine and had fathered a child of my own when the pain I had long suppressed once again reared its ugly head. I remember the day well: I had spent a year relishing the joys of fatherhood with my beautiful baby daughter, Nia. On this particular afternoon, a stunning realization suddenly overcame me: There was no way I could ever leave my helpless little girl in the care of anyone else for an extended period of time, much less for ten years. I recalled the cavernously empty feeling of missing my mother when I had come in first in my class, when my grandmother had harshly disciplined me in a way that I felt my mother would not have, or when I felt sad and alone and simply needed a hug. The painful memory of feeling abandoned was so overwhelming that I had to call my mother and ask her why, and more importantly, how it was possible that she could pick up and leave her family—leave us, leave *me*—when she did.

At first there was a long silence. She then took a deep sigh before replying that she absolutely had not wanted to leave us and that it was the most difficult thing she had ever done. She explained that given the deep poverty we lived in in Jamaica, the opportunity to go to the United States was a lifeline she felt she had to take. She had left not because she didn't love us, but because she loved us so much. As she spoke, we were both at the point of tears. I finally realized how difficult the decision had been for her to give up those early years with her children as we learned to talk and read, gained a sense of humor, made friends, learned new sports, and matured. While I had for many years suffered from feelings of abandonment, I had not once stopped to consider that she may have suffered even more. I could never have properly appreciated the depth of her sacrifice until I became a parent and understood just how immensely difficult it must have been for her. Understanding my painful past (and my mother's) required my living in a faraway future where I had a child of my own and was finally capable of empathizing with a decision made over a quarter century before.

I have used retrograde analysis many other times in my life. When I was around eighteen years old, I read two books that changed my life. The first was *Sugar Blues* by William Dufty, which details the hazardous effects of a diet containing too much white sugar and other refined foods. After reading it, I immediately gave up soda, ice cream, and candy and focused on natural foods and lean meats. The second book was *Passages* by Gail Sheehy, which describes the predictable crisis points of a man's life, beginning with the youthful twenties and going through his fifties and beyond. The book was essentially a road map of the future with detailed examples of the likely effects the aging process would have on my life.

At the time, both books scared the snot out of me. Still, I was grateful because they made me think about the quality of life I would like to have as I got older and how best to behave while I was young to achieve that goal. In other words, they taught me to live life backward.

One of the main techniques of a retro thinker is visualization, the ability to paint a vivid mental picture of the future in order to influence one's behavior in the present. I remember teaching this idea to the actor Will Smith in our very first chess lesson together. I told him to put the pieces where he wanted them to be, not where it seemed they could actually go: "Don't start by telling yourself what it can't be. Let your mind go fully to the impossible dream of where they could be. Put them where you want them. And now, one move at a time, you move backward to figure out how to get there."

Many well-known celebrities have been using this powerful visualization technique for years. Oprah Winfrey, dreaming of playing Sofia in the movie *The Color Purple*, recalls spending months and months visualizing herself as an actress and telling anyone who would listen to her that she was going to find a way to be in that movie. Jim Carrey, the comedian and actor, went as far as to sign a check to himself for $10 million, and dated it for five years from that moment, even though at the time he was dead broke. Shortly before the check came due, he found out that he had landed the role in the hit movie *Dumb and Dumber* . . . for $10 million! Arnold Schwarzenegger, former governor and action star, once said, "What you do is create a vision of who you want to be—and then live that picture as if it were already true."

The fact that we cannot accurately predict the future shouldn't stop us from using it to influence our behavior in the present. You could wonder, "How can I use the mindset of my future self to assist the actions of my current self?" It may seem difficult or even impossible, but it is much simpler than you might suppose. The key word in the question is *mindset*. Notice that the question is not "How can I use the *knowledge* of my future self to assist the actions of my current self?" Instead, the word *mindset* indicates that a mental shift will occur based on the knowledge of future events that may profoundly affect the person you will become. What's the evidence for this? It's in you right now! You are the future that your past self has evolved into.

There are many ways to prime our mindset for gaining "future" wisdom. We can start by looking at ways our strongest opinions have changed over time. We can also recall the most difficult things that have happened in our life and explore the insights we have gained from them. We can anticipate major events we know will occur in the near and distant future and imagine how we would feel if those things happened right now. Projecting our future from how we've navigated the past can help us navigate the journey forward.

Of course, it also makes sense to tap into the futures that have already been lived by others. Just as chess players study classic games of past masters to gain insights about their current play, studying classic texts that have stood the test of time is another sure way of gaining "future" wisdom. There is a reason why certain books have remained relevant for as long as they have, and even if they haven't held up entirely over the years, their cultural influence remains so large that they continue to resonate in people's minds and actions. The insights gained from great books tell us a lot about human behavior and psychology, no matter how much time has passed since they were written.

You can similarly tap into the wisdom and experiences of the current generation of our elders. Whether it's parents, aunts and uncles, teachers, or family friends, those who came immediately before us have essentially lived the future that we will experience. They already have some valuable opinions on life's biggest questions: What makes a true friend? What is your biggest regret, and how does it affect you now? How do you feel about death and dying? Would you change anything about your life if you had a chance? Their answers to these questions may provide valuable perspective.

It's important to note that the purpose of retrograde analysis is not necessarily to discover a detailed map to a specific answer—it can simply be a thinking tool to broaden your potential options by prompting you to look at a problem in a counterintuitive way. It also does not eliminate the need to think forward. In fact, the proof that you've arrived at a solution is that the path forward has become clear. By thinking of the inevitable future as a springboard, we can help address issues from our past and motivate ourselves to change our lives for the better in the present.

To Become, Be

"What you get by reaching your goals is not nearly so important as what you become by reaching them."

—ZIG ZIGLAR

"If you can meet with Triumph and Disaster
And treat those two impostors just the same . . ."

—RUDYARD KIPLING

One of the most painful losses I have ever had in a chess tournament was at the 1998 Bermuda International. I was playing against German grandmaster Michael Bezold. If I had won this particular game, I would have secured the points needed to earn the title of grandmaster myself. There came a critical moment where I had a choice between two moves: One was to take a rook with my bishop, and the other was to take a pawn in the middle of the board. Under time pressure, I chose to grab the rook. It turned out that the move threw away my entire advantage and gave my opponent fantastic attacking chances. Soon after, I ended up making another crucial mistake, which led to my defeat. I felt completely demoralized as my dream of getting the grandmaster title—seemingly so close at hand—went up in smoke.

After the game, Grandmaster Alexander Shabalov, who had been watching from a distance, approached me to discuss the fateful moment when I had greedily taken the rook. In a consoling tone, he pointed out that capturing the tiny but important pawn would have been the better choice. He then said to me words that I will never forget: "In order to become a grandmaster, you must first be a grandmaster."

It was one of those "Mr. Miyagi advising an over-eager student" moments. Shabalov was telling me that by trying too hard to get the title, by thinking too much about the points I needed, I was missing key parts of the process trying to get to the destination faster. I suddenly understood what my actual goal should have been all along: to simply embrace everything it took—studying and practicing, combined with stepping into the jungle of competition—to get as good as I possibly could. I didn't have to be stressed by constantly eyeing my ranking and trying to prove myself, letting doubts hamper my performance. I just had to be myself each and every day, to remain authentic to the journey and let the rest take care of itself. The games I played were simply a reflection of the work I was putting in. There was no need to worry about getting the points someone else had decided it would take to become a grandmaster. I just had to be one.

I spent the next year dedicating myself to chess. It became my whole life as I worked eight to ten hours a day studying not just the nuances of the game but the psychological battles I fought against my opponents and especially against myself. I dove deeper into the martial art of aikido to understand how to accept aggression with a calm spirit, and I practiced meditation to learn to maintain control of my ever-fidgety mind. I drew inspiration from books on great African Americans, such as baseball legend Jackie Robinson and tennis great Arthur Ashe, and I studied spirit-affirming books like Deepak Chopra's *Seven Spiritual Laws of Success* and *The Chicken Soup for the Soul* series by Jack Canfield and Mark Hansen. I was trying hard to become a better chess player first and foremost, but in the process, I slowly grew into a better version of myself.

The next opportunity I had at the title was at an international tournament held at the venerable Manhattan Chess Club in New York. I drew my first-round game, and then disaster struck in the second when I lost a terrible game, on my birthday no less. Suddenly the odds of getting the points I needed became daunting, as I would need to put together a difficult win streak against stiff opposition. After some deep soul-searching that evening with my great friend Willie Johnson, I turned things around and scored four and a half points in the next five games. All I needed to score my final grandmaster norm—and get the title—was a total of six points, and suddenly I was only one win away with two games to go. If I won my next game, the last one wouldn't matter.

On the afternoon of the eighth round, I was a nervous wreck. Despite managing the pressure leading up to that moment, my nerves felt as if they were threatening to strangle me as my childhood dream and the weight of history were staring me in the face. I remember ironing my shirt before the game and suddenly getting hit by a phrase my late grandmother used to turn on me: "jack of all trades, master of none." As a young child, I had often taken this as her scolding me for having a variety of interests, flitting like a bee from activity to activity with no sense of purpose or direction. As an adult, I would often say the phrase to myself in critical moments, feeling as though it were some sort of burden or curse that stopped me from accomplishing my goals. However, for some reason, as I held the iron suspended in the air, I suddenly realized that my grandmother had been saying those words out of love, that she had been trying to impart the lesson that mastery demanded purpose, focus, and determination. The realization stunned me, and I dropped the iron and started crying. Years of guilt and self-recrimination poured out of me as I let go of the anger I had at the woman who had raised me and who had simply tried to teach me as well as she could with the tools she had.

It took me some time to pull myself together. I went to the game, still unsettled by the experience, but at one moment, on move 14, I suddenly felt an incredible sense of calm. I could clearly and confidently see that if I didn't become a grandmaster by winning this game or the next one, I would simply do so at another tournament. In an instant, I lost the sense of desperately wanting the title and felt free to just play the chess position in front of me. A few moves later, when the choice came to return a pawn to my opponent or fight to keep it, I did the opposite of what I had done in the game against Bezold. This time, instead of clinging to the material, I sacrificed a pawn and trusted the power of my active pieces. As my attacking forces hovered over my opponent's position, he blundered badly. I paused and smiled before making the winning move. It seemed as though the universe were playing a joke. The killer move was so easy that even an amateur player would have seen what to do. I was about to secure the highest title in chess with a beginner's play.

All the hard work, the highs and lows, and the painful twists and turns that had brought me to that point had crystallized in the simplest of tactics. I made the move, embracing the past that had shaped me and stepping into the future that I had become. I would now receive the title of grandmaster. After all, I already was one.

Endgame

"Chess is the gymnasium of the mind."
—PETER PRATT

"Don't give your children the benefits of your success. Give them the ingredients that made you successful."
—PAUL ADEFARASIN

Chess teaches many more lessons than those covered in this book: The ability to stay calm under massive pressure. The skill of using another person's aggression to your advantage. The need for rest and recovery. The discipline to challenge our ideas in a systematic way. The list goes on and on.

Maybe the greatest lesson that chess teaches is humility. It may seem that the best players are untouchable in their brilliance, but the one thing that even the greatest chess minds know is that the game's complexity makes it a puzzle inside a mystery inside an enigma. It has remained unsolved for over fifteen hundred years and thankfully will continue to be for many more to come because its richness is virtually unfathomable. We continue to play because the human mind relishes a challenge, and we revel in the joy of play. This is how we learn best.

Hopefully, after reading this book, you feel inspired to break out a chess set and play. No matter your level, the game has something profound to teach. And even if you never pick up a chess piece in your life, I hope the lessons in this book—gleaned from my decades joyfully studying this infinitely fascinating game—will enrich you the way they've enriched me. The great American inventor and diplomat Benjamin Franklin put it best when he wrote, "The game of Chess is not merely an idle amusement. Several very valuable qualities of the mind, useful in the course of human life, are to be acquired or strengthened by it, so as to become habits, ready on all occasions."

Thirty-two pieces and pawns living inside sixty-four squares have entranced millions of people with uncountable hours of magic and adventure. Win or lose, each new game brings another captivating world full of exciting possibilities to explore. The battles never end, even after we hear "Checkmate." Then the quest to defeat our opponent and find ourselves begins anew.

ACKNOWLEDGMENTS

THIS BOOK would have been impossible without the support of many people who I am grateful to have in my corner.

A special thank you to my dear friend Anna Andrzejewska, who not only tirelessly read and reread the manuscripts, but who did so while patiently helping me with many of my other projects as well. I could not ask for a better friend.

Another special thank you to Sabina Foisor, who came on board just when I needed her, and gamely held down the fort by keeping my other initiatives on track while I was madly focused on getting to the finish line.

To everyone at Chronicle and especially my editor Allison Adler, whose level of patience I tested more than anyone's should be. Thanks for allowing me to find my own way.

To my mom, dad, and amazing siblings Devon, Sherill, Frank Jr., and Alicia. I won the lottery being born into such an amazing family.

To all my great friends at the St. Louis Chess Club, who rekindled my career and made so much of my success possible. Rex and Jeannie, your generosity will leave an indelible mark on world chess.

NOTES

Page 12: *Carlos Alcaraz says chess helps him:* Adam Addicott. "Carlos Alcaraz on How Playing Chess Helps Him Prepare for Matches." Ubitennis. August 3, 2022. https://www.ubitennis.net/2022/03/carlos-alcaraz-on-how-playing-chess-helps-him-prepare-for-matches/.

Page 13: *"Boxing is like chess":* Tracy Ramsden. "Nicola Adams: 'Women Boxers Focus on the Win Not the Trash Talk.'" *The Guardian* (UK edition). January 11, 2014. https://www.theguardian.com/lifeandstyle/2014/jan/11/nicola-adams-this-much-i-know.

Page 13: *a recent* Washington Post *headline:* Hannah Natanson. "Teachers Nationwide are Flummoxed by Students' New Chess Obsession." April 15, 2023. https://www.washingtonpost.com/education/2023/04/15/school-chess-class-clubs/.

Page 22: *"Advanced performers are unconsciously competent":* Scott Eden. "Stroke of Madness." *ESPN The Magazine.* January 22, 2013. https://www.espn.com/golf/story/_/id/8865487/tiger-woods-reinvents-golf-swing-third-career-espn-magazine.

Page 33: *"Whatever situation you drop him in":* Susan Ninan. "Anatomy of a GOAT: What Makes Magnus Carlsen the World's Best Chess

Player." ESPN. December 10, 2021. https://www.espn.com/chess/story/_/id/32840390/magnus-carlsen-world-champion-best-chess-player.

Page 79: *The late, great Kobe Bryant:* Lewis Howes. "Kobe Bryant: What Does Losing Feel Like to You?" YouTube. September 9, 2018. https://www.youtube.com/watch?v=MiO87miyyz4.

Page 83: *"There's no failure in sports"*: NBA on ESPN. "Giannis Was Asked if This Season Was a Failure after Playoffs Elimination." YouTube. April 26, 2023. https://www.youtube.com/watch?v=uZwlAzr44ys.

Page 94: *"I could throw in the towel"*: "Michelle Kwan's Fallen 131K Times—and We Could All Use Her Method to Getting Up." Shine. May 8, 2018. https://advice.theshineapp.com/articles/michelle-kwans-fallen-131k-times-and-we-could-all-use-her-method-to-getting/.

Page 94: *"You have to make mistakes"*: Anne Lamott. "Becoming the Person You Were Meant to Be: Where to Start." *O, The Oprah Magazine*. November 2009. https://www.oprah.com/spirit/how-to-find-out-who-you-really-are-by-anne-lamott/all.

Page 108: *Carlsen spoke about the mindset:* Tarjei Svensen. "'Good Outcome' to Face Nepo Not Fabi or Ding." Chess24. November 20, 2021. https://chess24.com/en/read/news/carlsen-good-outcome-to-face-nepo-not-fabi-or-ding.

Page 134: *As Magnus Carlsen put it:* "Magnus Carlsen Says People Fear Me." Offserpill Chess Club. YouTube. April 11, 2023. https://www.youtube.com/watch?v=WtRu8bRJLP0.

Page 139: *As Grandmaster Daniel Naroditsky describes it:* Daniel Naroditsky. "The Knockout Blow." Chess.com. November 28, 2014. https://www.chess.com/article/view/the-knockout-blow.

ABOUT THE AUTHOR

© Carlos Kremmer

MAURICE ASHLEY is a Chess Grandmaster, a chess commentator, a national championship coach, and an author. In 1999 he earned the title of Chess Grandmaster, making him the first African American Grandmaster in the game's history, and in 2016 he was inducted into the US Chess Hall of Fame. He lives in Florida.